Kingfisher

Learning Adventure Library

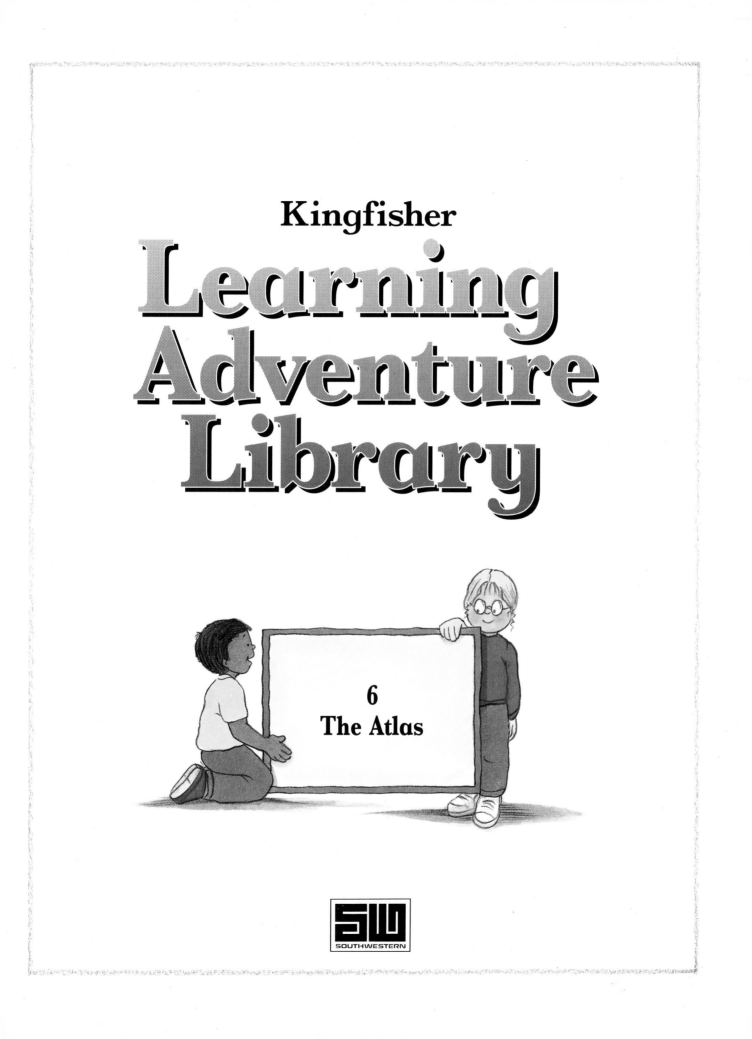

6
The Atlas

SW
SOUTHWESTERN

This edition published in 1996 by
The Southwestern Company
P.O. Box 305140
Nashville, TN 37230
by arrangement with Larousse plc
First published by Larousse plc 1994

Library of Congress Cataloging-in-Publication Data
available from Library of Congress

ISBN 0-87197-445-2

Printed in Italy

Editor: Catherine Headlam
Designers: John Jamieson and Terry Woodley
Consultant: Keith Lye
Additional research by Andrea Moran and Michael Butterworth
Map illustrations by Eugene Fleury (all political maps and the climate
map); John Woodcock (all picture maps)
Additional illustrations by Maggie Brand (Maggie Mundy Illustrators
Agency); Stephen Conlin; Jeremy Gower (B. L. Kearley Ltd.); Janos
Marffy (Kathy Jakeman Agency): Adam Marshall; Josephine Martin
(Garden Studio); Ralph Orme; Clare Roberts (Garden Studio);
Roger Stuart; Joanna Williams (B. L. Kearley Ltd.)

Contents

About this Atlas

Most of the world's land is divided up into seven large continents. In this atlas, six of the continents are shown twice. The first map shows all of the independent countries within each continent. [An independent country is one with its own government.] And the second map shows the major rivers, lakes, and mountains. The seventh continent, Antarctica, has just one map. This is because people don't live there all year round.

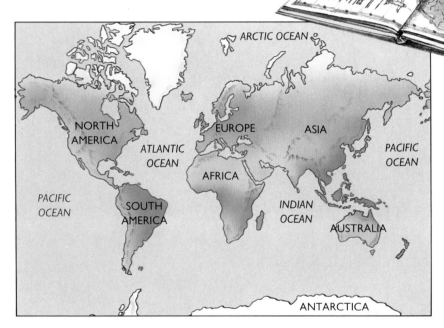

About the maps

On the first maps each country is clearly marked in a separate color with its capital city. The second maps are picture maps. They show the kind of animals that live on each continent, some of the plants that grow there, and the main industries. It is not possible, however, to show every spot where, for example, tigers or factories are found. There will be tigers and factories in other places besides those marked.

On the maps you will see where the biggest mountain ranges are, where the rivers flow to, what the names of the largest lakes are, as well as the names of the countries and their capital cities.

Each map has a scale. This will help you to work out how large the continent really is.

- Hills and mountains
- Country border
- Capital city
- Country
- River
- Important city

Where is it?

If you want to find a particular place in the atlas, look for it first in the index. After the place name you will see a page number and then a number and a letter, such as **4C**. This is the grid reference. Remember it as you turn to the page. Now look for the grid number (in a red circle) at the top and bottom of the page. There is a faint blue line running on either side of them, up and down the page. Now look for the letter, on the left- and right-hand sides of the page and the lines running beside these. You will find the place you are looking for in the square where the lines meet.

MAKING A MEAL OF IT

On the picture-map pages there is a box showing a typical meal from that continent, using the food that is grown there. Of course, people eat a huge variety of things in the different parts of any continent. None the less, each continent does have its own, individual kinds of food, and its own traditional recipes based on the common ingredients that are found in the region.

ANSWER THAT!

On all the map pages there is a box called "Answer That!" This asks you three questions about the map. You should be able to answer each of the questions by studying the map carefully. Look hard, and you are sure to find the solution—but some questions may require more looking than others! The correct answers to all the questions are given on page 38. Can you think of other questions to ask?

Where it comes from and where it is made

The picture maps include a series of symbols showing you the main products and industries of a region.

A factory marks an **industry** or industrial area, and logs marks the **lumber industry**. An oil rig shows where **oil** is drilled, and a flame shows **gas** production.

A mining wagon full of coal or metal, or two gemstones, show where **mining** takes place.

A beach umbrella and suitcase shows that the **tourist industry** is important in that area.

Large-scale **fishing** is represented by a trawler, and **animal farming** by a bull (for beef cattle), a dairy cow, a sheep, and a pig.

An ear of corn, a stalk of wheat, and a rice plant show where these important **cereals** are grown.

Various kinds of **fruit farming** are important in many parts of the world. These are shown by apples and pears, oranges and lemons, bananas, and grapes (which are also used to make wine).

Tea, coffee, and cocoa are important and valuable crops. These are shown by tea leaves, coffee beans, and cocoa pods.

Palm trees provide other crops such as copra from coconut palms (used to make coconut oil), dates from date palms, and palm oil.

Peanuts are sometimes known as groundnuts, and **sugar cane** is used to make sugar. Natural **rubber** is harvested from trees, and **cotton** comes from the fluffy seedheads of the cotton plant.

Factory

Lumber

Oil

Gas

Mining

Gemstones

Tourism

Fishing

Beef cattle

Dairy cows

Sheep

Pigs

Corn

Wheat

Rice

Apples and pears

Citrus fruits

Bananas

Grapes and wine

Tea

Coffee

Cocoa

Palm tree

Peanuts

Sugar cane

Rubber

Cotton

How maps are made

Maps are very clear and simple pictures of the world, so that we can see where places are, and how we might get from one place to another. Maps of the world are the result of years of work by navigators and surveyors who have visited the places and measured the shapes of land, the heights of mountains, the courses of rivers, and the position of towns and cities. In recent years, pictures from space satellites have helped to make maps even more accurate.

One of the big problems with maps of the world is that the world is not flat, but round.

To draw a flat map of the round world we have to cheat a little. Imagine the world as an orange.

Peel the skin off the orange, into segments of equal sizes. See how the segments are oval-shaped?

With the whole peel removed you have a true picture of the surface of the world divided into a row of oval segments.

But this does not make a very helpful map. So we cheat by stretching the Earth's surface to fill in the gaps between the segments to make a rectangle.

Map and scales

1. Using scale is a way of drawing places very much smaller than they are in real life, but still showing exactly where they are. If you are in Paris you can see the Eiffel Tower at its real size.

2. A map of the area around the Eiffel Tower will need to be drawn smaller than real size—to a smaller scale. So, for example, every inch on the map is equal to 600 feet of the real place or area.

0   600
feet

3. Maps can be drawn to any scale, depending on what they are trying to show. A map of Paris shows the area of the city and two sizes of roads, but cannot show the Eiffel Tower in detail.

Paris

4. With an even smaller scale, a map will show much less detail about the city itself, but more about the country around it. A map of France will simply show where Paris is placed in the country.

London
Amsterdam
BELGIUM Brussels
Luxembourg
Paris
Loire River
F R A N C E
Bern
Rhône River
ANDORRA
S P A I N
Barcelona **Corsica (France)**

Make your own map

Try making your own map of a place you know well, such as the area between your home and your school. Imagine how it would look from above. Draw in the streets, and show where all the main buildings are. Add any railroads, parks, rivers, and bridges. Keep the map as simple as possible by using symbols so that you can get more information into a small space. Could your friends use the map to find your home?

Railroad
School
Bridges
River
Park
Home

Climate and land

Every part of the world has its own climate or pattern of weather. It may be warm in summer, rainy in spring, and very cold in winter. Or it may be hot all year round. The climate of a country depends on the shape of its land, as well as its position in the world.

	Polar
	Cool and snowy
	Temperate
	Dry land and desert
	Tropical
	Mountain

This map of the world shows where the six main types of climate are found. Each climate is shown in a different color.

A **temperate climate** has warm summers and cool winters, and plenty of rain, which is good for farming.

SOME WORLD FACTS
Longest river the Nile River (4,160 miles)
Highest mountain Mount Everest (29,028 feet)
Highest waterfall Angel Falls, Venezuela (3,212 feet)
Largest country Russia (6.5 million square miles)
Smallest independent country the Vatican City State, in Italy (109 acres)
Largest continent Asia
Smallest continent Australia
Largest ocean the Pacific

The world can be divided into two halves by an imaginary line called the equator. The tropics form a band around the equator between two more imaginary lines called the Tropic of Cancer and the Tropic of Capricorn. The tropics receive the heat of the Sun from directly overhead. A **tropical climate** is hot and there is plenty of rain.

Cool and snowy climates are found around the polar regions. The Sun is never high in the sky in these areas and so the land receives less heat. The land may be frozen for months on end.

Tropic of Cancer

Equator

Mountain climates vary with the mountain's height. Most have quite a lot of rain or snow, but some are dry.

Tropic of Capricorn

Dry land and desert climates have low levels of rainfall. Deserts have almost no rain at all. Few plants can grow in these conditions.

A **polar climate** is bitterly cold, creating a thick layer of snow and ice. The North and South poles get warmth from the Sun only during their brief summer.

9

North America

Two English-speaking countries occupy most of North America: Canada and the United States of America. The third country, Mexico, is Spanish-speaking.

The United States is the world's richest and most powerful country. It is divided into 50 states.

To the south lies the warm Caribbean Sea, with hundreds of islands. A ribbon of land links North America to South America and contains a cluster of Spanish-speaking countries. Together these are known as Central America.

ATLANTIC OCEAN
ARCTIC OCEAN
PACIFIC OCEAN
INDIAN OCEAN

The Inuit (or Eskimo) people live in the very cold Arctic lands. In the past, they made houses called igloos from blocks of snow, and traveled on dogsleds. Now many live in towns and use motorized snowmobiles.

kilometers
0   400   800   1200   1600
0   200   400   600   800   1000
miles

Greenland is the largest island in the world. Although it is close to North America, its government is linked to Denmark. Most of the land is covered with snow and ice.

New York City is the largest city in the U.S.A. The huge Statue of Liberty stands on an island in New York Harbor.

St. Pierre et Miquelon (France)

Greenland (Denmark)

HUDSON BAY

C A N A D A

Mackenzie River

Yukon River

Saskatchewan River

Alaska (U.S.A.)

Canada is the second largest country in the world. The northern part is remote and empty. Most people live in the south, close to the U.S.A.

The Hawaiian Islands

Hawaii (U.S.A.)

The Hawaiian Islands lie about 2,360 miles (3,800 km) from the west coast of the U.S.A., in the Pacific Ocean. This group of islands forms the state of Hawaii. The islands are boxed to show that they are drawn closer to the mainland of the U.S.A. than they really are.

Washington

Washington D.C. is the capital of the U.S.A. It contains government buildings, such as the Capitol, where the U.S. Congress meets.

Mexico is a Spanish-speaking country with volcanoes and mountains, and long, sandy beaches. Its capital, Mexico City, is one of the largest cities in the world.

The Panama Canal was opened in 1914. Before then, ships had to sail all the way around South America to travel between the Pacific and the Atlantic oceans.

St. Kitts and Nevis are two small Caribbean islands, which together form the smallest independent country in North America.

For the capital cities of the smaller islands, look up the country name in the index.

ANSWER THAT!

1. Which country shares the southern border of the United States?

2. Which is the largest island in the Caribbean Sea?

3. Which island is called green, but is hardly green at all!

Map labels

PACIFIC OCEAN
ATLANTIC OCEAN
CARIBBEAN SEA
GULF OF MEXICO

UNITED STATES OF AMERICA
MEXICO

San Francisco
Los Angeles
Dallas
Chicago
Detroit
Boston
New York City
Philadelphia
Washington D.C.
Montreal
Ottawa
Toronto

GREAT LAKES
L. Superior
L. Huron
L. Michigan
L. Erie
L. Ontario
Saint Lawrence

Snake River
Columbia
Colorado
Missouri River
Arkansas River
Red River
Rio Grande
Mississippi River
Ohio River

Guadalajara
Monterrey
Mexico City

Bermuda (U.K.)

BAHAMAS
Nassau
CUBA
Havana
Cayman Islands (U.K.)
JAMAICA
Kingston
HAITI
Port-au-Prince
DOMINICAN REPUBLIC
Santo Domingo
Puerto Rico (U.S.A.)
San Juan

BELIZE
Belmopan
GUATEMALA
Guatemala City
HONDURAS
Tegucigalpa
EL SALVADOR
San Salvador
NICARAGUA
Managua
COSTA RICA
San José
PANAMA
Panama City
Panama Canal

Virgin Islands (U.S.A./U.K.)
Anguilla (U.K.)
ST. KITTS AND NEVIS
ANTIGUA AND BARBUDA
Guadeloupe (France)
Montserrat (U.K.)
DOMINICA
Martinique (France)
ST. LUCIA
BARBADOS
ST. VINCENT AND THE GRENADINES
GRENADA
Netherlands Antilles (Neth.)
TRINIDAD AND TOBAGO
Port-of-Spain

11

MAKING A MEAL OF IT

Every November Americans celebrate Thanksgiving by eating the traditional meal of turkey with cranberry sauce, sweet potatoes, and pumpkin pie.

The Great Lakes lie on the border between Canada and the U.S.A. and are linked to the Atlantic by the St. Lawrence River.

Beavers live in many of the smaller rivers of North America. They cut down young trees to build dams and homes called lodges. The dams block the streams and create small lakes.

Lumber is one of the most important products of Canada. The wood is made into planks and paper. The workers who cut down the trees are called lumberjacks.

Mount McKinley, in Alaska, is the highest mountain in North America. It rises to 20,321 feet (6,194 m) It is surrounded by the Denali National Park. (Denali is the Native American name for Mount McKinley).

GREENLAND

Polar bear

Harp seal

Right whale

Narwhal

Ringed seal

Puffin

Canada goose

Snow goose

HUDSON BAY

Beaver

Musk ox

Walrus

Arctic hare

Arctic wolf

Caribou

Mackenzie River

Moose

Rocky Mountain goat

Saskatche

Brown bear

ROCKY MOUNTAI

Yukon River

MOUNT McKINLEY

Bald eagle

Salmon

RUSSIA

The Mississippi and Missouri rivers together are about 3,730 miles (6,000 km) long—the longest river system in North America.

Corn has been grown in North America for thousands of years. It is eaten as a vegetable, and as popcorn or flour.

ANSWER THAT!

1. What is the name of the sea mammal with one long spiked tusk on its nose?

2. Which river forms part of the southern U.S. border?

3. Which "dog" is not a dog at all but lives in underground "towns?"

Sugar cane is grown in Central America, and on many Caribbean islands. The tall, thick stems are crushed to extract the clear, sweet juice, which is then made into sugar.

The Grand Canyon in Arizona is one of the great natural wonders of the world. It was created by the Colorado River, which has cut a narrow gorge through the rock. In some places it is nearly a mile (1.6 km) deep.

Sequoias growing in California are the largest trees in the world. The tallest is a giant sequoia that has grown to over 360 feet (110 m). Some sequoias are believed to be nearly 3,000 years old.

Lobster

Cape Canaveral

Hibiscus

Hummingbird

Helliconia

Quetzal

Coconuts

Rock beauty

Alligator

Raccoon

Black bear

GULF OF MEXICO

Cuban hogfish

APPALACHIAN MOUNTAINS

St. Lawrence River

L. Huron

L. Ontario

L. Erie

L. Michigan

L. Superior

GREAT LAKES

Mississippi River

Prairie dog

Skunk

Pelican

Red River

Arkansas River

Coyote

Rio Grande

Gila monster

Saguaro cactus

Missouri River

Bison

Kit fox

Rattlesnake

River

Colorado River

GRAND CANYON

Snake River

Monarch butterfly

Humpback whale

Gray whale

Dolphin

Swordfish

14

Brazil is by far the largest country in South America. Much of the land area is taken up by the basin of the Amazon River. Brazil is rich in iron, and produces more coffee than any other country.

French Guiana (or Guyane) is governed by France. European rockets are launched from its space station at Kourou (see page 16).

Surinam is the smallest independent country in South America. It was governed by the Netherlands until 1975.

Ecuador means equator in Spanish. Although the coasts are hot, the center of the country is high in the Andes, where the weather is cooler.

Rio de Janeiro has a huge statue of Jesus on a hill above the city. Nearby São Paulo is the biggest city in South America. It has a population of over 15 million.

Rio de Janeiro

South America

In the very south of South America the sea is ice-cold. But the shore of the north coast is on the warm Caribbean Sea. In between are the huge tropical forests around the Amazon River in Brazil, and the vast grassy plains called the Pampas in Argentina and Uruguay. The Andes run down the western side of South America. Originally the native peoples spoke many different languages. Then about 500 years ago, European settlers arrived and now most of the people of South America speak Spanish, except in Brazil, where the main language is Portuguese.

ATLANTIC OCEAN

| 0 | 200 | 400 | 600 | 800 kilometers |

| 0 | 100 | 200 | 300 | 400 | 500 miles |

Montevideo

URUGUAY

Uruguay River

Asunción

PARAGUAY

Paraná River

Buenos Aires

ARGENTINA

São Paulo

Santiago

ANDES MOUNTAINS

CHILE

Falkland Islands (U.K.)

CAPE HORN

Punta Arenas

Punta Arenas is farther south than any other city in the world.

La Paz is the world's highest capital city, standing 11,900 feet (3,627 m) above sea level. The air is thin at this height, and visitors from other lower countries can feel quite breathless.

Machu Picchu is a ruined city of the ancient Inca people. It lies high in the mountains of Peru and remained hidden for hundreds of years before it was rediscovered in 1911.

ANSWER THAT!

1. How many countries in South America begin with the letter B?

2. What is the name of the longest and thinnest country in South America?

3. Which country has coasts on the Pacific Ocean and on the Caribbean Sea?

15

16

ANSWER THAT!

1. Which South American animal likes to hang upside down from branches?

2. One animal likes to eat ants, which it picks up with its sticky tongue. What is its name?

3. Which frog can be used to make poison arrows?

The Amazon River is 4,007 miles (6,448 km) long (slightly shorter than the Nile River in Africa). However, it carries far more water than any other river in the world, and 60 times more than the Nile.

Cocoa is grown in the warm parts of South America. Chocolate is made from the seeds, or beans, that are found inside the cocoa pods.

The Angel Falls is the highest waterfall in the world. The water tumbles from a height of 3,212 feet (979 m).

Lake Titicaca is the largest freshwater lake in South America. It is 12,506 feet (3,812 m) above sea level. The ferry service across the lake is the world's highest

CARIBBEAN SEA

PACIFIC OCEAN

GUIANA HIGHLANDS

Orinoco River

Rio Negro

Japurá River

Madeira River

Amazon River

Xingu River

Tocantins River

São Francisco River

Marañón River

Ucayali River

LAKE TITICACA

Giant leatherback turtle

Surinam road

ANGEL FALLS

Macaw

Howler monkey

Kapok tree

Harpy eagle

Brazil nut tree

Poison arrow frog

Anaconda

Capybara

Spider monkey

Llama

Sloth

Piranha

Manatee

Kourou

Kinkajou

Hummingbird

Giant anteater

Toucan

Tarantula

Marmoset

Soccer is a favorite sport all over South America. Brazil was the first country to win the World Cup three times.

The Pampas covers much of Argentina and Uruguay. Large herds of beef cattle are raised on these huge grassy plains. They are looked after by cowboys called gauchos.

MAKING A MEAL OF IT
Many of our common foods come originally from Central and South America. These include corn, tomatoes, and potatoes. A common meal in South America consists of beef with boiled rice or potatoes, tomatoes, and slices of fried plantain (a fruit like a banana).

Elephant seals are the largest of all seals. They live in cold waters and breed on the shores of southern Argentina. Male elephant seals can be as much as 20 feet (6 m) long.

The Atacama Desert is one of the driest places on Earth. Some parts of it have gone 400 years without rain.

Condors are large vultures that live in the Andes. Some have a wingspan of over 10 feet (3 m). They feed on the bodies of dead animals.

The Andes form the longest mountain range in the world. They stretch for 4,500 miles (7,250 km). The highest peak is Aconcagua, which rises to 22,830 feet (6,959 m).

ATLANTIC OCEAN

ATACAMA DESERT

Jaguar

Uruguay River

Para

Paraná River

Guinea pig

Rhea

▲ ACONCAGUA

Vicuña

Chinchilla

Monkey puzzle tree

Armadillo

Patagonian hare

Fur seal

Elephant seal

CAPE HORN

Magellan penguin

Blue whale

17

Europe

There are more than 40 countries in Europe, and about as many languages. This is a wealthy part of the world with many old, historic cities and lots of big industries producing cars, chemicals, medicines, and other products. It generally has mild weather, with plenty of rain, which is good for farming. Southern Europe, around the Mediterranean Sea, has very warm summers, while the north is cooler with long, cold, and dark winters.

Brussels is the capital of Belgium. It is also the headquarters of the European Union (or EU). It has 12 member nations: Belgium, Denmark, France, Germany, Greece, Ireland, Italy, Luxembourg, the Netherlands, Portugal, Spain, and the United Kingdom.

Paris is the capital of France and one of the largest cities in Europe. Its many famous buildings include the Eiffel Tower, a huge metal tower built in 1889.

| 0 | 200 | 400 | 600 | 800 kilometers |
| 0 | 100 | 200 | 300 | 400 | 500 miles |

For the capital cities of the smallest countries, look up the country name in the index.

ICELAND
Reykjavik

Faeroe Islands (Denmark)

ATLANTIC OCEAN

NORTH S

REPUBLIC OF IRELAND
Dublin
IRISH SEA

UNITED KINGDOM
London

ENGLISH CHANNEL

NETHERLANDS
Amster

BELGIUM
Brussels

Rhine

LUXEMBOURG
Paris
Luxembo

Loire River

BAY OF BISCAY

FRANCE

SWITZERLA

Rhône River

Po R

ANDORRA

MONACO

PORTUGAL

SPAIN

Ebro River

Madrid

Barcelona

Cor (Fran

Lisbon

Tajo River

Sardi (Italy

Strait of Gibraltar

Gibraltar (U.K.)

MEDITERRANEAN SEA

ARCTIC OCEAN

ATLANTIC OCEAN

PACIFIC OCEAN

INDIAN OCEAN

The Vatican City State is the smallest country in the world. It lies inside the city of Rome. The Vatican is the headquarters of the Roman Catholic Church, which is led by the Pope.

NORWEGIAN SEA

ANSWER THAT!

1. Which country earned its name because it is so icy? (Clue: it is an island).
2. Which city in which country is in both Europe and Asia?
3. Which country in Europe begins with the letter C, but does not have any sea around its borders?

Oslo
Helsinki
St. Petersburg
Stockholm
Tallinn
ESTONIA
RUSSIA
Riga
LATVIA
NMARK
Copenhagen
LITHUANIA
Vilnius
Moscow
Minsk
Kaliningrad (Russia)
BELARUS
Berlin
Warsaw
RMANY
Prague
CZECH REPUBLIC
Kiev
UKRAINE
River
SLOVAKIA
Vienna
Bratislava
AUSTRIA
MOLDOVA
HTENSTEIN
Budapest
Chisinau
HUNGARY
jubljana
Zagreb
ROMANIA
VENIA
CROATIA
YUGOSLAVIA
Belgrade
SAN MARINO
Sarajevo
Bucharest
BLACK SEA
CASPIAN SEA
me
BOSNIA-
HERZEGOVINA
Sofia
ICAN
Y STATE
Skopje
BULGARIA
Tirana
Istanbul
Istanbul is the largest city in Turkey. Most of Turkey is in Asia, but a small part of it is in Europe. Istanbul lies in both Europe and Asia.
ALBANIA
TURKEY
MACEDONIA
ly (Italy)
Athens
Valletta
MALTA
Crete (Greece)

N. Dvina River
Ural River
Don River
Volga River
Dnepr River
BALTIC SEA
POLAND

Moscow is the capital of Russia, and one of the largest cities in Europe. St. Basil's Cathedral is so colorful that it looks as though it might be made of candy—but it is not!

19

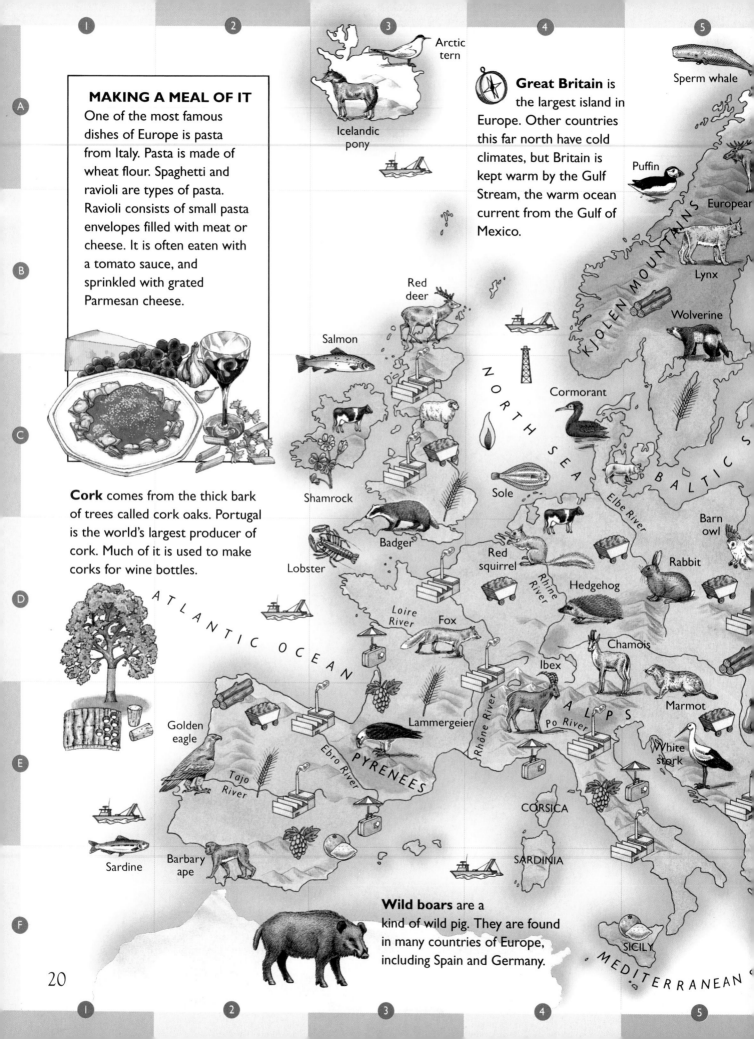

MAKING A MEAL OF IT

One of the most famous dishes of Europe is pasta from Italy. Pasta is made of wheat flour. Spaghetti and ravioli are types of pasta. Ravioli consists of small pasta envelopes filled with meat or cheese. It is often eaten with a tomato sauce, and sprinkled with grated Parmesan cheese.

Cork comes from the thick bark of trees called cork oaks. Portugal is the world's largest producer of cork. Much of it is used to make corks for wine bottles.

Arctic tern

Icelandic pony

Great Britain is the largest island in Europe. Other countries this far north have cold climates, but Britain is kept warm by the Gulf Stream, the warm ocean current from the Gulf of Mexico.

Sperm whale

Puffin

European

Lynx

Wolverine

KJOLEN MOUNTAINS

Red deer

Salmon

NORTH SEA

Cormorant

BALTIC

Sole

Elbe River

Barn owl

Shamrock

Red squirrel

Rabbit

Badger

Hedgehog

Lobster

Rhine River

Loire River

Fox

Chamois

Ibex

Marmot

ATLANTIC OCEAN

Lammergeier

Rhône River

A L P S

Po River

White stork

Golden eagle

Ebro River

PYRENEES

Tajo River

CORSICA

SARDINIA

Sardine

Barbary ape

Wild boars are a kind of wild pig. They are found in many countries of Europe, including Spain and Germany.

SICILY

MEDITERRANEAN

A

Gray seal

Polar bear

URAL MOUNTAINS

Reindeer

Wolf

N. Dvina River

Ptarmigan

B

Brown bear

Jay

ANSWER THAT!
1. A big fish-eating bird beginning with the letter P lives around the Black Sea. What is its name?
2. Where do you need to watch out for wolves and bears?
3. Where can you find a mountain goat-antelope beginning with the letter C?

Trout

C

Demoiselle crane

Ural River

The Volga River is the longest river in Europe. It flows 2,194 miles (3,531 km) through Russia to the Caspian Sea.

Weasel

Dnepr River

Don River

Steppe eagle

The Caspian Sea is a salt-water lake—the largest lake in the world. There, fish called sturgeon produce the eggs we know as caviar, one of the world's most expensive foods.

D

Volga River

Pelican

Sturgeon

C A S P I A N   S E A

Suslik

CAUCASUS

CARPATHIAN MOUNTAINS

MOUNT ELBRUS ▲

MOUNTAINS

E

Danube River

B L A C K   S E A

Rose

Mount Elbrus is the highest mountain in Europe, rising to 18,510 feet (5,642 m). It is part of the Caucasus range, very close to Asia.

Squid

Bread is an important food and comes in many different varieties in Europe. It is usually made from wheat or rye flour. The bubbles in the bread come from adding yeast, which makes the dough rise.

F

CRETE

Russia is the largest country in the world. About one fifth of it lies in Europe, and the rest is in Asia.

Russia is the largest country in the world. About one fifth of it lies in Europe, and the rest is in Asia.

Moscow

Mecca, in Saudi Arabia, is the most holy city of the Muslims. This is where the Prophet Muhammad was born. Every year over 500,000 pilgrims from around the world visit Mecca's main mosque.

Asia

Asia is by far the largest of the seven continents. It stretches from the warm seas around the equator to the Arctic Circle, and includes hot deserts, freezing cold wastelands, and the Himalayas, the highest mountains in the world. China and India both have huge populations. Most of the people live around the edge of the continent, and much of the center and north is remote and empty. Although Asia has many poor people, it also includes some of the world's richest countries.

The Maldives are a group of about 2,000 islands. Together they form the smallest country in Asia. It is also the world's flattest country.

E A N

6

BERING SEA

8

Aleutian Islands (U.S.A.)

Lena River

LE BAIKAL

■Ulan Bator

O L I A

Harbin ●

Amur River

Vladivostok ●

NORTH KOREA

Pyongyang ■

Seoul ■

Beijing ■

SOUTH KOREA

ng He River

Shanghai ●

EAST CHINA SEA

Yangtze (Chang Jiang) River

Wuhan ●

Chonqing ●

Taipei ■

TAIWAN

Guangzhou ●

Hong Kong (U.K.)

Macao (Portugal)

■Hanoi

ntiane

LAOS

AND

ngkok

AMBODIA

'hnom
'enh'

SOUTH CHINA SEA

PHILIPPINES

● Manila

SEA OF JAPAN

JAPAN

Tokyo ●

P A C I F I C   O C E A N

BRUNEI■ Bandar Seri Begawan

MALAYSIA

■Kuala Lumpur
SINGAPORE

IRIAN JAYA

Equator

I N D O N E S I A

■Jakarta

6

7

8

0   400   800   1200   1600 kilometers

0   200   400   600   800   1000 miles

9

10

A

The Trans-Siberian Railroad is the longest in the world. The 8-day journey from Moscow to Vladivostok covers over 5,000 miles (9,000 km).

B

Japan is made up of four main islands. Its capital, Tokyo, is among the biggest cities in the world. Japan produces cars, computers, toys, and many other products, which have made it one of the world's leading industrial nations.

C

Hong Kong is a tiny British territory on the coast of southern China. It is one of the world's great business centers with a very busy port. In 1997 Hong Kong will become part of China again.

D

China has a population of over a billion people. Most of them live in the eastern part of the country, where there are many big cities and good farmland.

ANSWER THAT!

1. What is the largest country in Asia (and also the largest country in the world)?

2. What is the capital of India?

3. Which country in Southeast Asia was named after King Philip II of Spain?

E

F

23

9

10

ANSWER THAT!
1. What is the correct name for a camel with two humps?
2. In which country can you find tigers?
3. Most rhinoceroses live in Africa, but there are small numbers in Asia as well. Where might you find one?

The Arabian Peninsula is almost entirely hot, dry desert. Most of the peninsula is occupied by Saudi Arabia, which has no rivers at all.

Oil is one of the main products of the Middle East, the southwestern part of Asia. The oil comes from wells under the ground. It is made into gasoline and other products, such as Tarmac and plastics.

Mount Everest, in the Himalayas, rises to 29,028 feet (8,848 m) and is the highest mountain in the world. It was first climbed in 1953. All ten of the world's highest mountains are in the Himalayas.

Siberia is a huge, cold region that covers most of Asian Russia. There are mountains and forests, and vast frozen wastes— and very few people.

Polar bear
Lemming
Reindeer
Ob River
Saiga antelope
URAL MOUNTAINS
ALTA
MOUNTAIN
Sturgeon
Demoiselle crane
CASPIAN SEA
ARAL SEA
Irtysh River
Cedar of Lebanon
Goat
Euphrates River
Tigris River
Bactrian cam
Yak
Oryx
ARABIAN PENINSULA
RED SEA
Onager
Lammergeier
MOUNT EVEREST
Indus River
HIMALAYAS
Camel
Dates
Tiger
ARABIAN SEA
Indian elephant
BAY OF BENGAL
Cobra
INDIAN OCEAN
Orangu

ARCT

A

B

C

D

E

F

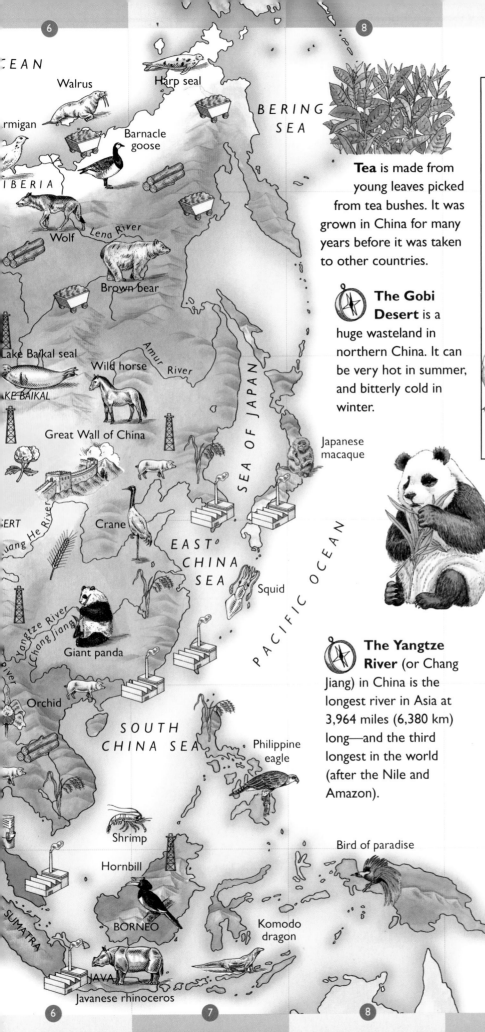

Walrus

Harp seal

BERING SEA

rmigan

Barnacle goose

IBERIA

Wolf

Lena River

Brown bear

Lake Baikal seal

Wild horse

Amur River

KE BAIKAL

Great Wall of China

SEA OF JAPAN

Japanese macaque

ERT

uang He River

Crane

EAST CHINA SEA

Squid

PACIFIC OCEAN

Yangtze River
Chang Jiang

Giant panda

Orchid

SOUTH CHINA SEA

Philippine eagle

River

Shrimp

Hornbill

Bird of paradise

SUMATRA

BORNEO

Komodo dragon

JAVA

Javanese rhinoceros

Tea is made from young leaves picked from tea bushes. It was grown in China for many years before it was taken to other countries.

The Gobi Desert is a huge wasteland in northern China. It can be very hot in summer, and bitterly cold in winter.

The Yangtze River (or Chang Jiang) in China is the longest river in Asia at 3,964 miles (6,380 km) long—and the third longest in the world (after the Nile and Amazon).

MAKING A MEAL OF IT

The food of southern Asia is famous for its spicy flavors. Spices include ginger, cumin, coriander, cinnamon, pepper, yellow turmeric, and hot red chilies. The Indian dish called lamb korma is cooked with yogurt and contains all these spices. It can be served with rice or bread.

Giant pandas are found in the forests of southern China. Bamboo is their main food. Although they are a protected species, there are very few pandas still living in the wild.

Rice is the most important food of South and East Asia. The rice plant is a kind of grass. It is usually grown in flooded fields, called paddies.

3

Tunis

Algiers

Rabat

TUNISIA

Tripoli

El Aaiun

WESTERN SAHARA

MOROCCO

ALGERIA

LIB

SAHARA DES

MAURITANIA

MALI

NIGER

CH

Timbuktu in Mali was once a rich city trading in gold. For many early European explorers in Africa it was the most exciting and distant place they could think of.

CAPE VERDE

Nouakchott

Niger River

Timbuktu

Niamey

Dakar

Senegal River

SENEGAL

Banjul

Bamako

BURKINA FASO

N'Djam

Chari R.

GAMBIA

Bissau

Ouagadougou

NIGERIA

GUINEA-BISSAU

Conakry

GUINEA

TOGO

BENIN

Abuja

Freetown

CÔTE D'IVOIRE

GHANA

Lomé

Lagos

SIERRA LEONE

LIBERIA

Abidjan

Accra

Porto-Novo

Malabo

CAMEROON

CENTR

Bangui

Monrovia

Yaoundé

Mosques can be seen in many parts of Africa, particularly in North and West Africa, where most people are Muslims.

ATLANTIC OCEAN

SÃO TOMÉ AND PRINCIPE

São Tomé

Libreville

EQUATORIAL GUINEA

GABON

CONGO

Ubang

Brazzaville

Kinsha

Cabinda (Angola)

Luanda

Africa

The second biggest continent after Asia is Africa. It lies across the equator, so all African countries have a warm climate. North Africa is hot and dry, and most of its people live along the Mediterranean coast. They are separated from the rest of Africa by the Sahara Desert. Rain is more plentiful south of the Sahara and this allows tropical forests to grow in Central Africa. East Africa has drier grasslands. Many African countries are rich in diamonds, gold, and other metals. But in some areas the people are very poor and do not have enough to eat.

Markets in Africa are lively and colorful places, where people can buy almost anything—from meat, vegetables, spices, and cooking oil to cloth, shoes, and toys. Usually the markets are run by women.

ANG

NAMIB

Windhoe

Johannesburg is the largest city in South Africa. It developed as the center for the goldmining industry. South Africa is the world's largest producer of gold.

Cape Tow

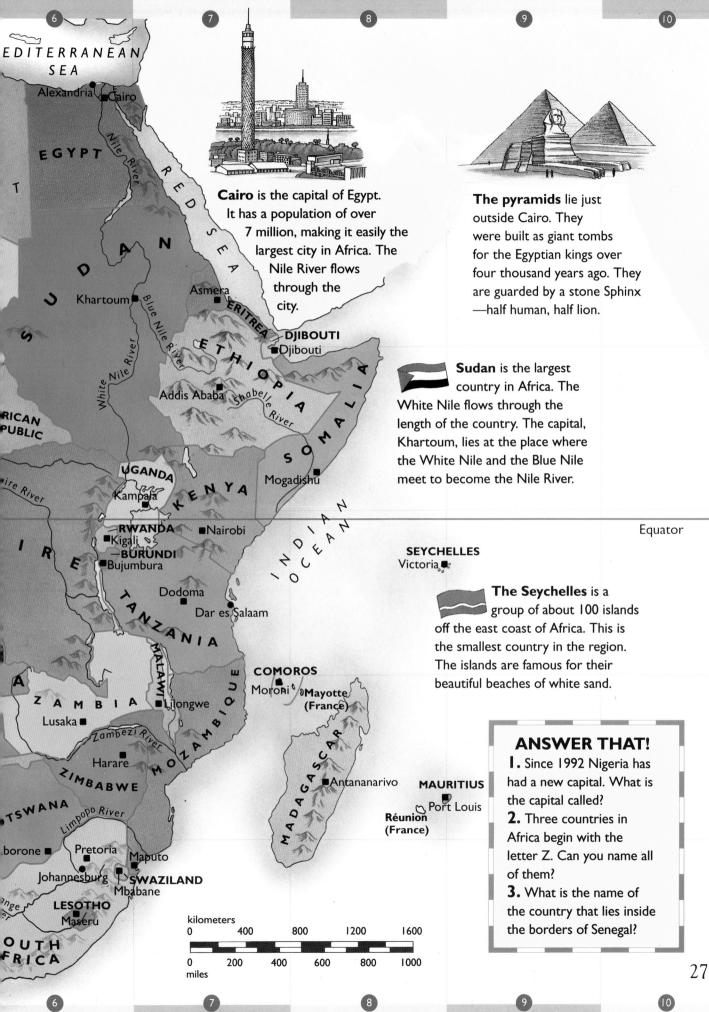

MEDITERRANEAN SEA

Alexandria ■ ■Cairo

E G Y P T

T

Nile River

RED SEA

SUDAN

Khartoum ■

Blue Nile River

Asmera ■

ERITREA

White Nile River

DJIBOUTI
■Djibouti

E T H I O P I A

Addis Ababa ■

Shabelle River

S O M A L I A

RICAN PUBLIC

Mogadishu ■

ire River

UGANDA

Kampala ■

K E N Y A

■Nairobi

RWANDA
Kigali ■

■BURUNDI
Bujumbura

Dodoma ■

T A N Z A N I A

Dar es Salaam ■

I R E

MALAWI

Lilongwe ■

A

Z A M B I A

Lusaka ■

Zambezi River

Harare ■

Z I M B A B W E

M O Z A M B I Q U E

TSWANA

Limpopo River

borone ■

Pretoria ■

Maputo ■

Johannesburg ■

■SWAZILAND
Mbabane ■

LESOTHO
Maseru ■

nge

OUTH FRICA

I N D I A N   O C E A N

COMOROS
Moroni ● ●Mayotte (France)

M A D A G A S C A R

■Antananarivo

Equator

SEYCHELLES
Victoria ■●

MAURITIUS
● Port Louis

Réunion (France)

Cairo is the capital of Egypt. It has a population of over 7 million, making it easily the largest city in Africa. The Nile River flows through the city.

The pyramids lie just outside Cairo. They were built as giant tombs for the Egyptian kings over four thousand years ago. They are guarded by a stone Sphinx —half human, half lion.

Sudan is the largest country in Africa. The White Nile flows through the length of the country. The capital, Khartoum, lies at the place where the White Nile and the Blue Nile meet to become the Nile River.

The Seychelles is a group of about 100 islands off the east coast of Africa. This is the smallest country in the region. The islands are famous for their beautiful beaches of white sand.

ANSWER THAT!
1. Since 1992 Nigeria has had a new capital. What is the capital called?
2. Three countries in Africa begin with the letter Z. Can you name all of them?
3. What is the name of the country that lies inside the borders of Senegal?

kilometers
0   400   800   1200   1600

0   200   400   600   800   1000
miles

27

MAKING A MEAL OF IT

African cooking varies from region to region. In North Africa, the most famous dish is couscous—fluffy grains of steamed wheat. In West Africa, meat stews are often cooked with a spiced peanut sauce containing dried shrimps. (In Africa, peanuts are often called groundnuts.) The stews are eaten with sliced root vegetables, such as yams.

The Sahara Desert is the largest desert in the world. Much of it is covered by huge sand dunes, but in some areas there are high, rocky mountains. Camels are used to carry goods and people in desert areas.

ANSWER THAT!

1. What is the name of the lizard from Madagascar that can change color to match its background?
2. If you wanted to cross the Sahara Desert, what animal would you take to carry your baggage?
3. Which animal's name begins with two A's?

28

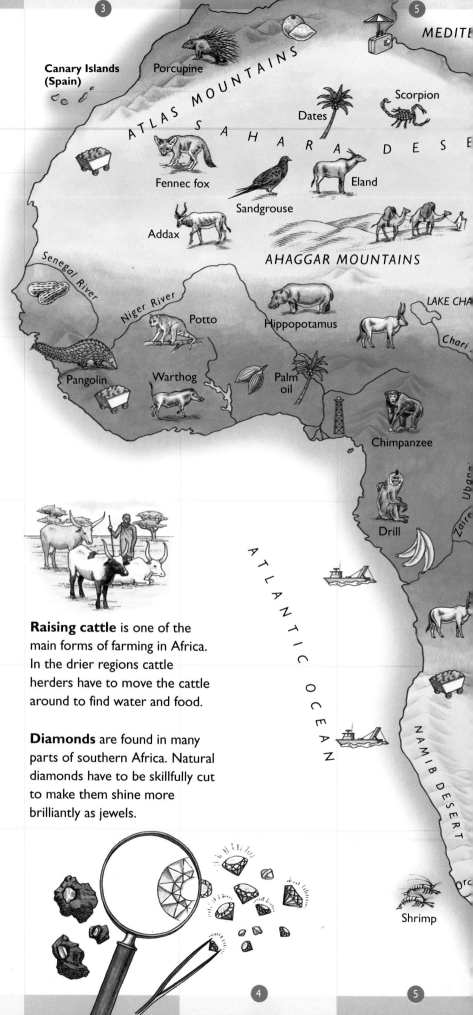

Raising cattle is one of the main forms of farming in Africa. In the drier regions cattle herders have to move the cattle around to find water and food.

Diamonds are found in many parts of southern Africa. Natural diamonds have to be skillfully cut to make them shine more brilliantly as jewels.

Canary Islands (Spain)

Porcupine

ATLAS MOUNTAINS

SAHARA DESE

Dates

Scorpion

Fennec fox

Sandgrouse

Eland

Addax

AHAGGAR MOUNTAINS

LAKE CHA

MEDITE

Senegal River

Niger River

Potto

Hippopotamus

Chari

Pangolin

Warthog

Palm oil

Chimpanzee

Drill

Ubang

Zaire

ATLANTIC OCEAN

NAMIB DESERT

Shrimp

Or

Coffee is made from the seeds of the coffee plant. It was probably first grown in Ethiopia.

The Nile River is the longest river in the world. It flows 4,145 miles (6,670 km) from its source at Lake Victoria to the Mediterranean Sea.

The African elephant is the largest living animal on land. Elephants can grow to over 10 feet (3 m) tall and weigh 6 tons. Some elephants live to over 70 years of age.

Lake Victoria is the largest lake in Africa, and the third largest lake in the world. It lies between three countries: Kenya, Tanzania, and Uganda.

Mount Kilimanjaro in Tanzania is the highest mountain in Africa. Its tallest peak rises to 19,340 feet (5,895 m) and is covered with snow throughout the year.

Madagascar is the largest island off Africa. Some of its wildlife is found only in Madagascar—such as the ring-tailed lemur, a relative of the monkey family.

Camel
Oryx
Leopard
Hornbill
Acacia tree
Nubian goat
Aardvark
Cheetah
Lion
LAKE VICTORIA
LAKE TANGANYIKA
MOUNT KILIMANJARO
Giraffe
Zebra
LAKE MALAWI
MADAGASCAR
Hyena
Gemsbok
Chameleon
Ring-tailed lemur
INDIAN OCEAN
Hartebeest
Wildebeest
Whale
Cape baboon
RED SEA
Nile River
Blue Nile River
White Nile River
Shabelle River
Zambezi River
Limpopo River
AN SEA

Grid markers: 1 2 3 4 5 (top), A B C D E (left side)

ANSWER THAT!
1. What is the capital of Australia?
2. The South Pacific islands are divided into three groups. There is Melanesia, and Micronesia. What is the third group called?
3. Which island of New Zealand is Wellington on?

Papua New Guinea makes up the eastern half of the island of New Guinea. The western half is Irian Jaya, a part of Indonesia. New Guinea is the second largest island in the world, after Greenland.

M I C R

PAPUA NEW GUINEA
Port Moresby
M E

The Aborigines have been living in Australia for over fifty thousand years. They once lived by gathering wild food and by hunting, and sometimes used boomerangs (left) to knock down their prey.

ARAFURA SEA

TIMOR SEA

Darwin

CORAL SEA

GREAT DIVIDING RANGE

Australia is the smallest of the seven continents. The word Australia means "Southern Land." It was given this name by the Europeans, who first came here about 350 years ago.

INDIAN OCEAN

A U S T R A L I A

Brisban

Darling River

Murray River

Perth

Adelaide

Sydney

Canberra

Melbourne

kilometers
0   400   800   1200   1600

0   200   400   600   800   1000
miles

TASMANIA

T A S M A N

Sydney is the largest city in Australia, with a population of over 3 million people. Its most famous building is the Opera House, built at the edge of its beautiful harbor. The roof of the Opera House looks like the sails of a ship.

For the capital cities of the smaller islands, look up the country name in the index.

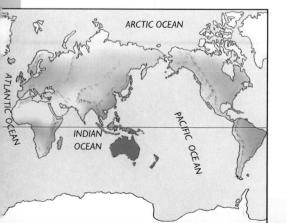

ARCTIC OCEAN

ATLANTIC OCEAN

INDIAN OCEAN

PACIFIC OCEAN

ARSHALL ISLANDS

Nauru is a tiny island which is just 8 square miles (21 sq km) in size. It is one of the smallest independent countries in the world.

The Polynesian islands lie in the middle of the South Pacific Ocean. Islanders used to travel vast distances between the islands in small sailing boats.

A

ESIA

DERATED ATES OF CRONESIA

PACIFIC OCEAN

Equator

NAURU

KIRIBATI

B

SOLOMON ISLANDS

P O L Y N E S I A

Honiara

TUVALU

Tokelau (N.Z.)

WESTERN SAMOA

Wallis and Futuna (France)

American Samoa (U.S.A.)

Apia

C

VANUATU

N E S I A

Vila

Suva

TONGA

Cook Islands (N.Z.)

French Polynesia (France)

FIJI

Niue (N.Z.)

ew Caledonia (France)

Nuku'alofa

D

New Zealand lies some 1,550 miles (2,500 km) rom Australia. It is made up of wo main islands. Most people ive on the North Island, where Auckland is the largest city.

Kermadec Islands (N.Z.)

Australia and the Pacific Islands

Australia is so big that it is called a continent. It is about the same size as the United States, without Alaska. The cities are all close to the coast. Inland, there are vast farms where sheep and cattle are raised, but most of central Australia is hot desert.

Like Australia, New Zealand is mainly English-speaking. Here the weather is mild, and snow falls on the mountains in winter. To the north is the Pacific Ocean, with thousands of warm, tropical islands. They include tiny islands, such as Nauru, which are among the smallest nations in the world.

E

EA

North Island

Auckland

South Island

Wellington

Christchurch

Chatham Island (N.Z.)

F

31

ANSWER THAT!

1. What color is the famous swan of Western Australia?

2. What is the name of the rock in the center of Australia?

3. New Zealand has two birds, whose names begin with K, neither of which can fly. What are they?

Mount Wilhelm in Papua New Guinea is the highest mountain in the region, rising to 14,793 feet (4,509 m). Mount Cook, in New Zealand, is another high mountain, at 12,350 feet (3,764 m).

Crowned pigeon

Fruit bat

MOUNT WILHELM

Coconuts

Bird of paradise

A R A F U R A   S E A

Crocodile

Taipan

Shrimp

C O R A L   S E A

GREAT BARRIER REEF

T I M O R   S E A

Grass tree

I N D I A N   O C E A N

GREAT SANDY DESERT

AYERS ROCK

Kookaburra

SIMPSON DESERT

Frilled lizard

MacDONNELL RANGES

GIBSON DESERT

Koala

Emu

GREAT VICTORIA DESERT

Lyrebird

Black swan

Wallaby

Darling River

Duck-billed platypus

Ring-tailed possum

Kangaroos are marsupials—animals that carry their young in a pouch.

Blue whale

Eucalyptus (gum) tree

The Darling River flows into the Murray River in Australia to form the longest river of the region. It is 2,330 miles (3,750 km) long.

Tasmanian devil

Shark

Sheep are important farm animals in both Australia and New Zealand. Some of the sheep and cattle stations (ranches) in Australia are as big as the country of Belgium. And there are about 18 times more sheep in New Zealand than there are people. Wool is sheared from the sheep to make cloth.

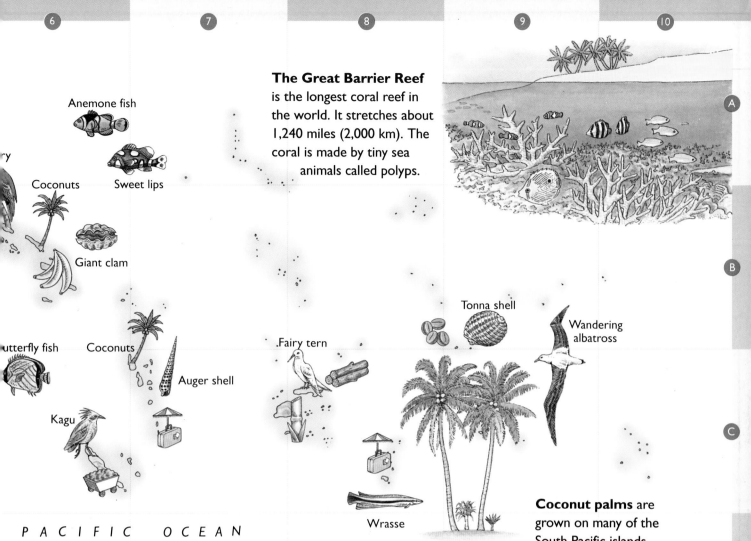

Anemone fish

Coconuts Sweet lips

Giant clam

The Great Barrier Reef
is the longest coral reef in
the world. It stretches about
1,240 miles (2,000 km). The
coral is made by tiny sea
animals called polyps.

utterfly fish Coconuts

Kagu

Auger shell

Fairy tern

Tonna shell

Wandering
albatross

Wrasse

Coconut palms are
grown on many of the
South Pacific islands.

P A C I F I C   O C E A N

Tuna

Geysers gush up from the
ground at Rotorua, New
Zealand. They are like
fountains of hot water. The
water is heated by volcanic
activity under the ground.

MAKING A MEAL OF IT
The warm weather of
Australia is ideal for eating
outdoors, and Australians
love to have barbecues. They
cook large steaks, as well as
lamb, fish, and shrimp. For
dessert they can have home-
grown fruit, such as bananas,
kiwifruit, pineapple, peaches,
and watermelon.

Tuatara

T A S M A N   S E A

•Rotorua

Kakapo

Takahe

Shrimp

MOUNT
COOK

Kiwi

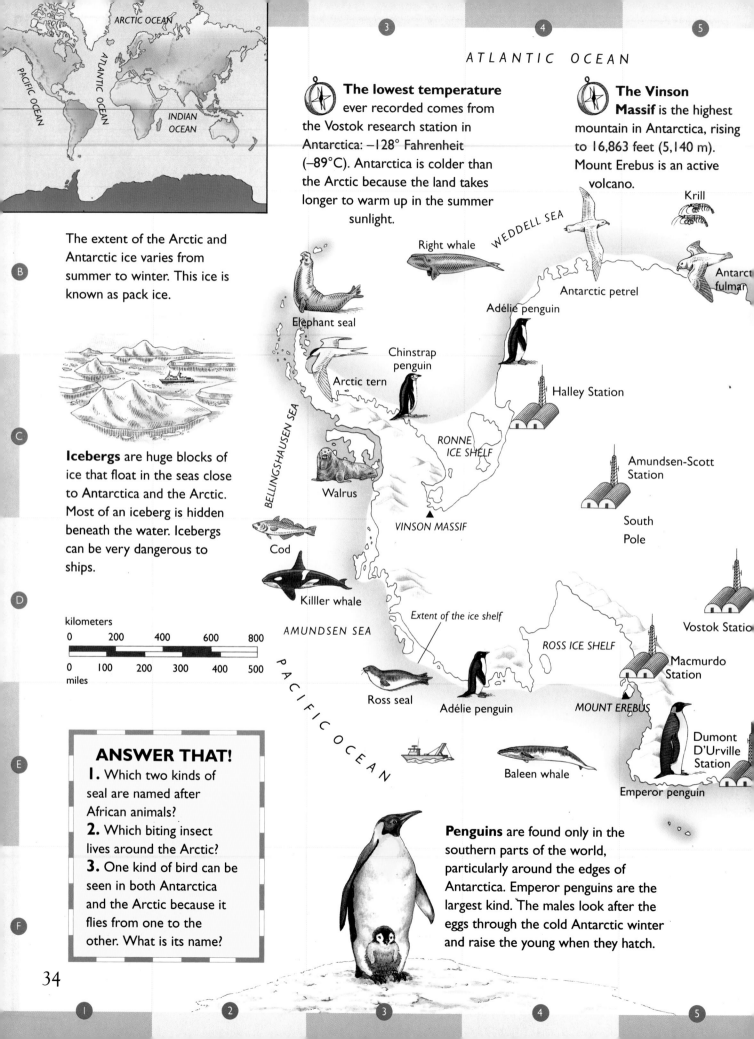

ARCTIC OCEAN

PACIFIC OCEAN

ATLANTIC OCEAN

INDIAN OCEAN

B The extent of the Arctic and Antarctic ice varies from summer to winter. This ice is known as pack ice.

C **Icebergs** are huge blocks of ice that float in the seas close to Antarctica and the Arctic. Most of an iceberg is hidden beneath the water. Icebergs can be very dangerous to ships.

D

kilometers
0   200   400   600   800

0   100   200   300   400   500
miles

E

F

ANSWER THAT!
1. Which two kinds of seal are named after African animals?
2. Which biting insect lives around the Arctic?
3. One kind of bird can be seen in both Antarctica and the Arctic because it flies from one to the other. What is its name?

34

The lowest temperature ever recorded comes from the Vostok research station in Antarctica: −128° Fahrenheit (−89°C). Antarctica is colder than the Arctic because the land takes longer to warm up in the summer sunlight.

ATLANTIC OCEAN

The Vinson Massif is the highest mountain in Antarctica, rising to 16,863 feet (5,140 m). Mount Erebus is an active volcano.

Krill

Right whale

Antarctic petrel

Antarctic fulmar

Adélie penguin

Elephant seal

WEDDELL SEA

Chinstrap penguin

Arctic tern

Halley Station

RONNE ICE SHELF

BELLINGSHAUSEN SEA

Walrus

Amundsen-Scott Station

Cod

VINSON MASSIF

South Pole

Killer whale

Extent of the ice shelf

ROSS ICE SHELF

Vostok Station

AMUNDSEN SEA

Macmurdo Station

PACIFIC OCEAN

Ross seal

Adélie penguin

MOUNT EREBUS

Baleen whale

Dumont D'Urville Station

Emperor penguin

Penguins are found only in the southern parts of the world, particularly around the edges of Antarctica. Emperor penguins are the largest kind. The males look after the eggs through the cold Antarctic winter and raise the young when they hatch.

CANADA

Walrus

Husky

GREENLAND

Arctic poppy

Mosquito

NORWAY

Sperm whale

Ptarmigan

Caribou

Arctic fox

Arctic tern

ARCTIC OCEAN

North
Pole

Alaska (U.S.A.)

Squid

Cod

Extent of the ice pack

Gray whale

Mawson Station

Barnacle goose

Long-tailed skua

Crab-eater seal

| 0 | 400 | 800 | 1200 | 1600 kilometers |

| 0 | 200 | 400 | 600 | 800 | 1000 miles |

Arctic wolf

Polar bear

RUSSIA

South Polar
skua

INDIAN OCEAN

Casey Base

Scientific stations carry
out research in various parts
of Antarctica, usually during
the short summer. The
scientists study such things
as weather patterns and
animal life.

...pard seal

Antarctica and the Arctic

The very top and bottom of the world
are the places that receive the least
sunlight, and in winter they get no
sunlight at all. These regions are bitterly
cold and covered with thick layers of ice and snow.
The farthest point south on our planet is called the
South Pole, and the farthest point north is called
the North Pole.

The South Pole is actually on land, in the middle
of the continent called Antarctica. The North
Pole is not on land at all, but on a huge sheet of ice
in the middle of the Arctic Ocean. The size of the
ice sheet changes as the ice melts and freezes
during the year. Neither Antarctica nor the
Arctic is owned by any country, and the only
people living there are explorers and scientists.

Flags of the World

North America

CANADA

UNITED STATES OF AMERICA

MEXICO

GUATEMALA

BELIZE

EL SALVADOR

HONDURAS

NICARAGUA

COSTA RICA

PANAMA

BAHAMAS

CUBA

JAMAICA

HAITI

DOMINICAN REPUBLIC

ANTIGUA AND BARBUDA

ST. KITTS AND NEVIS

DOMINICA

ST. LUCIA

BARBADOS

GRENADA

ST. VINCENT AND THE GRENADINES

TRINIDAD AND TOBAGO

South America

VENEZUELA

GUYANA

SURINAM

BRAZIL

COLOMBIA

ECUADOR

PERU

BOLIVIA

PARAGUAY

URUGUAY

CHILE

ARGENTINA

Europe

ICELAND

NORWAY

SWEDEN

FINLAND

DENMARK

IRELAND

NETHERLANDS

BELGIUM

LUXEMBOURG

FRANCE

MONACO

SPAIN

ANDORRA

PORTUGAL

ITALY

SAN MARINO

VATICAN CITY STATE

UNITED KINGDOM

SWITZERLAND

LIECHTENSTEIN

AUSTRIA

GERMANY

POLAND

CZECH REPUBLIC

SLOVAKIA

HUNGARY

SLOVENIA

CROATIA

BOSNIA-HERZEGOVINA

MALTA

MACEDONIA

ALBANIA

GREECE

BULGARIA

ROMANIA

RUSSIA

ESTONIA

LATVIA

LITHUANIA

BELARUS

UKRAINE

YUGOSLAVIA

MOLDOVA

SYRIA

IRAN

LAOS

INDONESIA

COTE D'IVOIRE

ERITREA

Asia

GEORGIA

LEBANON

AFGHANISTAN

VIETNAM

Africa

MALI

ETHIOPIA

ARMENIA

ISRAEL

PAKISTAN

CHINA

MOROCCO

BURKINA FASO

DJIBOUTI

AZERBAIJAN

JORDAN

INDIA

MONGOLIA

ALGERIA

GHANA

SOMALIA

KAZAKHSTAN

SAUDI ARABIA

NEPAL

NORTH KOREA

TUNISIA

TOGO

KENYA

TURKMENISTAN

YEMEN

BHUTAN

SOUTH KOREA

MAURITANIA

BENIN

UGANDA

UZBEKISTAN

OMAN

BANGLADESH

JAPAN

SENEGAL

NIGERIA

TANZANIA

TAJIKISTAN

UNITED ARAB EMIRATES

SRI LANKA

TAIWAN

GAMBIA

NIGER

BURUNDI

KYRGYZSTAN

QATAR

MALDIVES

PHILIPPINES

GUINEA-BISSAU

CHAD

RWANDA

BAHRAIN

BURMA (MYANMAR)

BRUNEI

GUINEA

LIBYA

ZAIRE

TURKEY

KUWAIT

THAILAND

MALAYSIA

SIERRA LEONE

CENTRAL AFRICAN
REPUBLIC

EGYPT

CYPRUS

IRAQ

CAMBODIA

SINGAPORE

LIBERIA

SUDAN

CAMEROON

37

EQUATORIAL GUINEA

LESOTHO

MARSHALL ISLANDS

GABON

SWAZILAND

SOLOMON ISLANDS

SAO TOME AND PRINCIPE

MADAGASCAR

NAURU

CONGO

CAPE VERDE

TUVALU

ANGOLA

SEYCHELLES

KIRIBATI

ZAMBIA

COMOROS

VANUATU

MALAWI

MAURITIUS

FIJI

MOZAMBIQUE

Australia and the Pacific

TONGA

ZIMBABWE

PAPUA NEW GUINEA

WESTERN SAMOA

BOTSWANA

AUSTRALIA

NAMIBIA

NEW ZEALAND

SOUTH AFRICA

FEDERATED STATES OF MICRONESIA

ANSWER THAT!

page 11
1. Mexico
2. Cuba
3. Greenland

page 13
1. Narwhal
2. Rio Grande
3. Prairie dog

page 15
1. Two, Brazil and Bolivia
2. Chile
3. Colombia

page 16
1. Sloth
2. Giant anteater
3. Poison arrow frog

page 19
1. Iceland
2. Istanbul in Turkey
3. Czech Republic

page 21
1. Pelican
2. Northern Russia
3. Chamois, in the Alps

page 23
1. Russia
2. New Delhi
3. Philippines

page 24
1. Bactrian camel
2. India
3. Java (Indonesia)

page 27
1. Abuja (it used to be Lagos)
2. Zaire, Zambia and Zimbabwe
3. Gambia

page 28
1. Chameleon
2. Camel
3. Aardvark

page 30
1. Canberra
2. Polynesia
3: North Island

page 32
1. Black
2. Ayers Rock
3. Kiwi (the national symbol of New Zealand) and Kakapo

page 34
1. Leopard seal and elephant seal
2. Mosquito
3. Arctic tern

Now you have answered all these questions, here are some other kinds of questions to ask.

What is the capital of...?
Which is the largest country in...?
Which is the smallest country in...?
Where is the highest mountain in...?
Where is the longest river in...?

Index